THE BATHROOM GAMBLING BOOK

by

Russ Edwards & Jack Kreismer

RED-LETTER PRESS, INC.
Saddle River, New Jersey

THE BATHROOM GAMBLING BOOK
Copyright ©2005 Red-Letter Press, Inc.
ISBN: 0-940462-43-5
All Rights Reserved
Printed in the United States of America

For information address:

Red-Letter Press, Inc.
P.O. Box 393, Saddle River, NJ 07458
www.Red-LetterPress.com

ACKNOWLEDGMENTS

Consultant Extraordinaire:
Mike "Ace" Ryan

Project Development Coordinator:
Kobus Reyneke

Cover design and typography:
s.w.artz, inc.

Editorial:
Jeff Kreismer

Significant Others:
Roy Harry
Kathy Hoyt
Robin Kreismer
Jim & Rory Tomlinson

INTRODUCTION

A fascination with gambling is part of human nature, and when nature calls, you can bet there's no better companion than The Bathroom Gambling Book.

The jokers are wild in this compendium of gaming humor and bar bets, and we've left nothing to chance by including a full house of terrific trivia, notes and quotes.

As the song says, "you've got to know when to hold 'em, know when to fold 'em" and whether you're going for broke, prepared to drop a bundle, or playing for peanuts, sit in for a few laughs... Odds are Lady Luck won't be the only one smiling.

And always remember, in life, as in poker, when you drop all your chips in the pot, you best back it up with a royal flush.

Here's wishing you an ace-in-the-hole.

Jack "The Joker" Kreismer
Publisher

FOR AMERICA'S
FAVORITE READING ROOM

THE BATHROOM GAMBLING BOOK

*A Light-hearted,
Lavatorial Look
at the Games People Play*

THE BATHROOM LIBRARY

RED-LETTER PRESS, INC.
Saddle River, New Jersey

"Gamblers are like toilets -
 broke one day and flush the next."

-Jack Kreismer

When cards were first printed in America, the manufacturers wanted nothing to do with anything representing England (such as kings and queens) so they substituted other figures. George Washington was the President of Hearts. Ben Franklin was the King of Clubs, Lafayette the King of Spades and John Adams was the King of Diamonds.

Herb comes home from work and excitedly says to his wife, "Pack the suitcases right away!"

"Why, what happened?" she asks.

"I just won a million bucks in the lottery!" Herb exclaims.

"Terrific!" says the wife. "Where are we going?"

"We're not going anywhere. You're leaving."

"If I lose today, I can look forward to winning tomorrow, and if I win today, I can expect to lose tomorrow. A sure thing is no fun."

-Chico Marx

"Trust everyone-and always cut the cards."

-W.C. Fields

The New York State Lottery suspended play on the number 3569 before noon on December 27, 1989, because it had been chosen by too many people. This was the number of the license plate (VR3569) on the truck New York Yankees manager Billy Martin was killed in a few days earlier.

Bar Bets

THE MATCH GAME

Find a willing victim and bet him that he can't break a match. Once he takes the bait, er, bet, put a match across the back of his middle finger and under the first and third finger at the joints nearest to the fingertips. Now he has to snap the match by pushing up his middle finger and pushing down with the other two. It's impossible to break at that point because that's where your fingers are weakest. After endless trying, offer to break it for him. Put it in the same position only further up the fingers (near the knuckles) and see how the match flies.

CHANCE REMARKS

"I believe in luck. How else can you explain the success
of those you dislike?"
-Jean Cocteau

"True luck consists not in holding the best of the cards
at the table: Luckiest is he who knows just when to rise
and go home."
-John Hay

"I'll never give up, for I may have a streak of luck before I die."
-Thomas Alva Edison

"Luck is a mighty queer thing. All you know about it
for certain is that it's bound to change."
-Bret Harte, American writer

"Fortune may have yet a better success in reserve for you,
and they who lose today may win tomorrow."
-Miguel de Cervantes, Don Quixote

"Luck sometimes visits a fool, but never sits down with him."
-German proverb

"For me dumb luck overcomes dumbness."
*-Bill Mayhew, $2 million
Maryland lottery winner*

"Regardless of the system you use, you've got to be lucky
to win. It's just pure luck."
-Sam Valenza, Jr., Lottery & Casino News

"In a bet there is a fool and a thief."

-Proverb

A guy walks into a bar and does a double take when he sees a horse serving the drinks.

"What the heck is this?" the guy demands.

The horse responds, "Look, mister. I've been having a rough go of it lately. A few years ago I won the Kentucky Derby. It was all downhill from there. My filly left me for some other stud. I had problems with my feet so they retired me. This was the only job available to me."

The guy was flabbergasted - a genuine Mr. Ed!

He asks the horse if the owner is around. The horse points to the kitchen. The guy goes into the kitchen and says to the bar owner, "I'd love to buy your horse."

The owner says, "A hundred bucks and he's yours. That horse is the worst bartender I've ever seen."

The guy say, "A hundred bucks?...Sold!"

The owner says, "Before we shake on it, I've gotta come clean with you. No matter what that horse tells you...he never won the Kentucky Derby."

Bar Bets

ELEVENS TO BETSY!

All right, the challenge here is to write the number eleven thousand, eleven hundred and eleven in just five seconds. Go! Well you know that it's really 12,111 but will they realize it in just a few seconds? It'll be fun finding out.

The Poker Hall of Fame was founded in 1979. The first seven inductees were: Johnny Moss, Nick "The Greek" Dandalos, Felton "Corky" McCorquodale, Red Winn, Sid Wyman, James Butler, "Wild Bill" Hickok, and Edmond Hoyle.

"If you can't quit when you're winning and won't quit when you're losing, that leaves only one logical time to stop - when you're broke."

-Tex Sheahan

"The race is not to the swift, nor the battle to the strong, but that's the way to bet."

-Grantland Rice

In 1945, President Harry S Truman (no period after the S because it doesn't stand for anything) played pot limit poker with the press corps sixteen hours a day aboard ship while coming home from the Potsdam Conference.

Ruppert Nerdock, the newspaper magnate, spent oodles of money to buy a racehorse. The noted trainer Willie Shumaker offered to race his horse against Murdock's. The night of the match race, the track was filled and sportswriters from all of Nerdock's newspapers were there. Unfortunately for Nerdock, his horse didn't live up to its billing and was beaten by nine lengths. The next day, the sports page headline on all of Nerdock's newspapers read:

NERDOCK'S HORSE FINISHES SECOND, SHUMAKER'S HORSE NEXT-TO-LAST.

Entertainer Groucho Marx earned his nickname because he always carried his poker winnings in a "grouch bag." He was a notorious cheat at the game.

Down in the High Rollers bar at the Blue Parrot Casino, an obviously inebriated man turned to the guy on the barstool next to him.

"Say, buddy, what's a 'breathalyzer' anyway?" he asked

"Well, it's this bag that tells you when you've had too much to drink," answered the equally wasted gent.

"Hey, whaddaya know? I've been married to one of those for years!"

"You got to know when to hold 'em, know when to fold 'em, know when to walk away, know when to run. You never count your money while you're sittin' at the table, there'll be time enough for countin' when the dealin's done."

-Kenny Rogers,
" *The Gambler*"

"Life consists not of holding good cards, but in playing those you do hold well."

-Josh Billings

Gambling generates more revenue than movies, spectator sports, theme parks, cruise ships and recorded music combined.

Otto was having a bad night at the blackjack table. His mood was so bad he began taking it out on the dealer.

When another player thanked the dealer and left a tip, Otto groused that it was nothing but a racket.

"You guys have nothing to do with whether players get good cards or bad," Otto growled. "Why do you expect a tip?"

"Well sir, a waiter serves you food and you tip him don't you?" the dealer replied.

"Yes but a waiter brings me what I want," countered Otto. "I'm sitting here with a thirteen- I'd like an eight."

TRICKS OF THE TRADE

If you're not having much luck at the craps table, you might want to try this roll of the dice on your friends.

Place three dice on the table and look the other way. Pick a volunteer, let's say in this case, Norm. "Norm, roll all three dice until you're satisfied with the numbers you get."

This is to make sure everyone watching knows that the dice are perfectly normal.

Then continue in a very deliberate fashion... "Norm, quietly add up the numbers on the faces. Pick up one of the dice and turn it over so that you can see the number on the bottom. Now, what I'd like you to do is add this number to your total. Finally, roll that same die and add the number on its face to the total."

Now its time for you to amazingly announce the total that Norm came up with.

It's surprisingly simple but seemingly astounding.

The opposite sides of a die always add up to seven. Here's how Norm reached his number: The two dice that Norm did not pick up are added together by you. With the die that Norm picked up, he was asked to add the top side to the bottom side. In other words, he added seven to his total.

Now you have the total of the two dice that were not picked up plus seven. When Norm rolled the die that he picked up that number was available to you, so you simply add seven to the total showing and- presto!- you've got the correct answer.

*"My advice to the unborn is, don't be born with
a gambling instinct unless you have a good sense
of probabilities."*

-Jack Dreyfus,
of the Dreyfus Mutual Fund

Alfredo Lim, Director of the National
Bureau of Investigation, was assigned by
President Corazon Aquino to investigate
charges of fixing at the Philippines state
lottery's September 1, 1990, drawing. At the
September 16th drawing, which was specially
televised in hopes of restoring public
confidence in the game, Lim stepped forward
with the winning ticket to collect the
$200,000 top prize.

*The wife of a prominent physician who was
attending a convention in Atlantic City phoned
the casino where she knew he'd be spending
most of his time and asked to have him paged.*

*"Sorry ma'am," she was told. "The house does
not make doctor calls."*

Every day this guy prays to God to let him win the lottery. He keeps promising to do all sorts of good deeds if God will only let him win the jackpot. Week after week he prays but never wins. Finally, one day he's talking to God and says, "I'm a good man. I've been praying faithfully. Can't you allow me to win the lottery?"

A booming voice from the heavens answers, "You gotta buy a ticket!"

George Washington was such an avid card player that he kept a record of his achievements in his diary.

Some of the earliest cards in America were made from the skins of sheep and deer.

"The urge to gamble is so universal and its practice so pleasurable that I assume it must be evil."

-Heywood Hale Broun

"I have always wondered if the results of the Versailles Conferences would have been different if Woodrow Wilson had been a poker player."

\- Clyde Brion Davis

The formal term for the house advantage in the gambling business is the vigorish, or vig for short.

Bar Bets

NICKEL PICKLE

Here's a bet that requires a steady hand and sharp scissors. Make a statement that you can trace a dime on a piece of paper, cut the hole out and drop a nickel through it. No way! Yes way! The secret is to fold the paper neatly in half, bisecting the hole. Place the nickel in the crease of the paper and very gently tug up on the ends of the cutout. The nickel will drop through.

A guy strolls into a butcher's shop and asks, "Are you a betting man?" The butcher answers, "Yes," so the guy says, "I'll bet you 100 bucks that you can't reach up and touch that meat hanging on the hooks up there." The butcher says, "No way... I'm not gonna take that bet. "But I thought you said you were a betting man," the guy retorts. "I am," responds the butcher, "but the steaks are too high."

In most casinos, the number 13 position will not be found at a baccarat table. We don't have to tell you why.

In 1978, Atlantic City, New Jersey, opened Resorts International, its first casino.

"A dollar picked up in the road is more satisfaction to us than the 99 which we had to work for, and the money won at Faro or in the stock market snuggles into our hearts in the same way."

-Mark Twain

"Nine gamblers could not feed a single rooster."

\- Yugoslav proverb

In 1963, Texas hold'em was first introduced in Las Vegas by Texan Felton "Corky" McCorquodale.

A Card Player's Secret To A Happy Marriage...

It's important to find a woman of tolerance who wants nothing more in the world than to please you and is willing to spend her last cent covering your losses.

It's important to find a woman who will massage your feet, clean your house and otherwise wait on you every waking moment, especially those nights when Lady Luck deserts you.

It's important that you find a gorgeous, lustful woman more than willing to disprove the old adage 'Lucky at cards, unlucky at love.'

And finally, it's really, really important that these three women never meet.

GOOD LUCK!

According to Zolar's Encyclopedia of Signs, Omens, and Superstitions, here are the luckiest days of the year:

January	July
4,19,27,31	2, 6, 10, 23, 30
February	August
7, 8, 18	5, 7, 10, 14, 19
March	September
3, 9, 12, 14, 16	6, 10, 15, 18, 30
April	October
5, 27	13, 16, 20, 31
May	November
1, 2, 4, 6, 9, 14	3, 13, 23, 30
June	December
3, 5, 7, 9, 12, 23	10, 20, 29

"My last piece of advice to the degenerate slot player who thinks he can beat the one-armed bandit consists of four little words: 'It can't be done.'"

-John Scarne

Sam: What'll you have, Normie?
Norm: Well, I'm in a gambling mood, Sammy.
*   I'll take a glass of whatever comes out of*
*   the tap.*
Sam: Looks like beer, Norm.
Norm: Call me Mister Lucky.
                                -TV's "Cheers"

In East Asia, jade is considered a symbol of power. Casino dealers are forbidden to wear any jade jewelry.

Benjamin Franklin printed and sold playing cards.

A chronic gambler comes home and finds his wife, a noted psychic, standing at the door with a rolling pin.

"You no-good louse," she growled, "and just where were you until 3 A.M. tomorrow morning?"

Bar Bets

WELL BLOW ME DOWN!

Bet them that they can't blow a strip of paper downwards.

Cut a regular piece of paper about a foot long and two inches wide. Have them hold it right under their lower lip. Blow down on the paper. See what happens! They can blow their brains out before they blow the paper down. It'll always rise up.

Two Martians were walking through a casino when they passed a slot machine that just hit the jackpot.

As great heaps of coins were disgorged all over the floor, one Martian patted the slot on the back and said, "You know, you ought to be in bed with a cold like that."

"Look high, look low, and we see that gamblers actually form the majority of the world's inhabitants."

-James Runciman

"Son, we are sorry about the tuition funds…
your mother and I didn't know you are not
supposed to split tens."

-A letter home from a couple
visiting Reno

Three men were waiting outside a hospital
delivery room. After a short while, a nurse came
into the waiting room and said,
"Congratulations, Mr. Smith, you're the proud
father of twins!"

"Well, what a coincidence," said Mr. Smith. "It
just so happens that I work for the Minnesota
Twins baseball team."

Later, the nurse came into the waiting room
again and said, "Congratulations, Mr. Johnson!
You're the father of triplets!"

"What a coincidence," said Mr. Johnson. "I
work for the 3-M Corporation!"

The third fellow in the waiting room got up to
leave. The nurse stopped him and said, "You
can't go yet. Your wife is still in the delivery
room. Why are you leaving now?"

The fellow said, "I gotta go find a second job
because I work for the Lucky 7 Dice Company."

CARD CAPERS

This is a simple, but very effective card trick. Pre-arrange the deck by stacking the four aces on top. Demonstrate that you are shuffling the deck, but make sure to leave the four aces on top. Now give the cards to anyone in your audience and instruct them to make as many separate "decks" as they'd like just so long as there are at least five cards in each pile. Meanwhile, be sure to keep track of the pile with the aces at the top. Once your victim is finished, move the top cards from each of the piles 'round and 'round, but not on top of the pile with the aces. After you've sufficiently completed that, take the pile with the aces and, one by one, put them on top of the decks. If there are more than four decks left, take the ones without the aces on top and put them underneath the piles with the aces. Next, tell your victim(s) that you're an "ace" at this … Flip over the top four cards to reveal all the aces in the deck.

The word "Ace," as in the playing card, comes from the Latin word "as" (pronounced ace).

"It can be argued that man's instinct to gamble is the only reason he is still not a monkey up in the trees."
                                    -Mario Puzo

"They gambled in the Garden of Eden, and they will again if there's another one."

-Richard Albert Canfield

About 150 couples get married in Las Vegas each day. The most popular wedding day in Sin City is Valentine's Day.

Wally and Theodore were talking about their favorite pastime- poker.

"How come you don't play poker with Clarence anymore?" Wally asked Theodore.

"Would you play poker with someone who was loud, obnoxious, drank all the beer and kept cheating?"

"No," replied Wally, "I certainly would not."

"Well," said Theodore, "neither will Clarence."

Harry was counting up the proceeds of the raffle he'd just held to benefit the Old Age Home For Destitute Gamblers when his friend Fred walked in.

"Wow!" said Fred, "That's a lot of dough."

"A quarter million dollars," replied Harry. "at 250,000 tickets which sold for a buck apiece."

"Gee, what was the prize?" asked Fred.

"A million bucks," Harry answered matter-of-factly.

"A million bucks? And you only sold a quarter of a million dollars in tickets? How did you plan to make money like that?"

"I never had a million dollars in the first place," answered Harry.

"But weren't they upset?" Fred asked incredulously.

"Only the guy who won," admitted Harry, "so I gave him his dollar back."

"A dollar won is twice as sweet as a dollar earned."

-Paul Newman, in
"The Color of Money"

"Gambling is an extension of child's play-the difference is that now we keep score with money."

-John Luckman

In the days of the Old West, a deck of cards was known as a "California prayer book" to a gambler.

Bar Bets

MAKE 'EM POP A CORK!

Start by filling a glass of water. Overfill it by adding water gently until the surface rises over the edge of the glass. Carefully place the cork afloat in the center. Now bet your buds that they can't keep it there. The water level is slightly lower at the rim and the cork will try to go downhill. Now bet that you can. Pour some of the water out until it's well under the rim and replace the cork. Now the water level at the rim is ever-so-slightly higher and the cork will again find the lowest point, this time in the center.

A craps player died and went to Heaven. Once up there, he was able to take a look down to Hell where he saw the most spectacular casino with a bunch of players standing around the craps table. "Boy, St. Peter," the gambler said. "It looks like they're just about to start. You call that Hell? I'd love to be playing there."

"That's the hell of it," smiled St. Peter. "So would they, but they don't have any dice."

There are 52 cards in a deck - four each of the ace, two, three, four, five, six, seven, eight, nine, ten, jack, queen and king. Oddly, the names spelled out collectively have exactly 52 letters!

"The Wampanoag Tribe has a machine, and they say, 'It's completely idiot proof.' I told them they've got it all wrong. I want a machine that is 'idiot friendly.'"

-Governor William F. Weld

"Sometimes nothing can be a real cool hand."

-Paul Newman, on poker, in
the movie "Cool Hand Luke"

Keno is one of the oldest gambling games, dating back to China almost 2,000 years ago. Originally, the game required one to pick 10 Chinese characters out of 120. The game was brought to the U.S. in the mid-1800s by Chinese laborers. Known then as the Chinese lottery, it was popular in many towns in the West but difficult for Americans to grasp. In 1936, the game was reduced to 80 Arabic numbers. Racehorse names were added to the numbers to make it legal in Nevada. It became known as "racehorse keno," later shortened to keno.

His horse lost the race, and the owner was beside himself. "I thought I told you to really turn it on at the end," he yelled at the jockey.

"I would have," responded the jockey, "but I didn't want to leave the horse behind."

HORSING AROUND

1. Name the three races in horse racing's Triple Crown.

2. What horse was nicknamed Big Red?

3. Who is the all-time winningest jockey?

4. When ESPN announced its list of the 50 greatest athletes of all time, what was the only nonhuman to make the grade?

5. Who was the oldest jockey to ever win the Kentucky Derby?

5. Willie Shoemaker, at the age of 54 in 1986.
4. Secretariat.
3. Laffit Pincay.
2. Secretariat.
1. The Kentucky Derby, the Preakness and the Belmont.

A jockey got hurt when he fell off his horse. He was rushed to a nearby hospital. A few hours later one of his colleagues phoned the hospital and asked the nurse how his buddy was doing.

She said, "Well, you're a jockey so you should know. He's in stable condition."

"One of the healthiest ways to gamble is with a spade and a package of garden seeds."

-Dan Bennett

"The next best thing to gambling, and winning, is gambling, and losing."

-Jimmy the Greek

The New Jersey Casino Control Commission requires casino slot machines to pay out at least 83 percent while in the state of Nevada, the Gaming Commission rules for slots to pay out a minimum of 75 percent. Actual payouts are much higher, however, as Nevada's payout is about 95 percent and Atlantic City's is around 91 percent.

A six-year-old horse was entered in a big money race and won by six lengths. The track manager contacted the owner and said, "Your horse is six years old and won by six lengths. Why haven't you entered him before?"

"We would have," replied the owner, "but we didn't catch up with him until last Wednesday."

"You should never challenge 'worse.' Don't ever say, 'Things couldn't get worse. Worse is rough... I was down to my last two hundred dollars. I mean, not to my name, but I lost all I could sign for. And I said, 'I'm gonna win something! It can't get worse.' I went over to the roulette wheel. And got two hundred dollars' worth of quarter chips. Covered the table - I mean covered the table! Red and black, even up. I'm going to win something before I go to sleep. And the guy spun the ball and it fell on the floor."

—Bill Cosby

Gambling ships must sail outside the 3-mile limit along the Atlantic Coast. They must sail at least 9 miles off the shores of the Gulf of Mexico before gambling becomes legal.

"I'm sorry I have not learned to play cards. It is very useful in life. It generates kindness and consolidates society."

- Samuel Johnson

"If there was no action around, he would play solitaire - and bet against himself."

-Groucho Marx,
about his brother Chico

Bar Bets

MENTAL MASTERY

Let's try using the power of the mind instead of trickery. Better yet, let's use the power of the mind to come up with more trickery.

Give your subject a penny and a nickel. They can place either coin in either hand. Now using the power of your mind (You were smart enough to read this book weren't you?), you'll divine the location of both coins.

To amplify the brain waves, your subject should be asked to think of twice the value of the coin in their left hand and don't give you the answer- just think. After a second or so, ask them to think about thirteen times the value of the coin in their right hand.

How long did they think? If it was instantaneous in both cases, the penny is in their left hand. Why? Because two times one or one times thirteen are extremely easy to calculate. If it took longer, then a safe bet is that the nickel is in the right hand because five times thirteen takes a little longer to figure out.

A guy hits the million-dollar jackpot on a slot machine in Vegas. As everyone crowded around to congratulate him, one disheveled looking guy said "Excuse me, but could you see your way clear to share your good fortune and give me $10,000 of your winnings? I could really use it to get my life back on track."

Touched but a bit wary, the winner replied, "But how do I know you won't just gamble it all away?"

So the other guy said "Hey, gambling money I got."

Megabucks was introduced to Nevada casinos in 1986 with a jackpot starting at $1 million. Terry Williams won the first jackpot, pocketing $4,988,842.14 from Harrah's in Reno.

"He once had a horse who finished ahead of the winner of the 1942 Kentucky Derby. Unfortunately, the horse started running in the 1941 Kentucky Derby."

-Groucho Marx

"There are two times in a man's life when he should not speculate; when he can't afford it, and when he can."

-Mark Twain

Some historians say the original design of the first roulette wheel was done by the noted French mathematician Pascal, who was experimenting with perpetual motion machines. The reason for their conclusion was based on the fact that Pascal gave the name "roulette" to the wheel he was experimenting with.

Clem: I've got good news and bad news.
Lem: What's the good news?
Clem: The guys got together and voted you
*   Most Valuable Player.*
Lem: What's the bad news?
Clem: It was at our weekly poker game.

A priest, a minister and a rabbi were playing cards one night when the police raided the game.

The cop asked the priest, who had just lost all his chips, if he'd been gambling.

"No, my son, I swear I haven't been gambling."

"Well, okay, I guess a priest wouldn't lie- you can go," said the cop.

Next he asked the minister who had no chips either, "Reverend, have you been gambling?"

"No I have not," answered the minister.

"Well I guess a minister wouldn't lie. You can go." said the cop.

Finally he turned to the rabbi who had all the chips and was holding a royal flush in his hand.

" Well now with all those chips and cards Rabbi, I think you're going to have to admit that you've been gambling."

"Gambling?" the rabbi asked. "With who?"

"I just played a horse yesterday so slow the jockey kept a diary of the trip."

-Henny Youngman

"Las Vegas has all kinds of gambling devices, such as dice, roulette, slot machines - and wedding chapels."

-Mike Ryan

In January 1963, actor Sean Connery, a.k.a 007 agent James Bond. was playing roulette at Casino de la Valle in Saint-Vincent, Italy. He played the number 17 three times in a row, each one coming up a winner! The actual odds of hitting the same number three times in a row are 50,653 to 1. Connery walked away with $30,000 in winnings.

A couple of gamblers were conversing. Said one to the other, "I lost $500 playing cards last night."

"Well, you're grinning from ear to ear. You don't seem to be too upset about it."

"I'm not. I was playing solitaire."

Bar Bets

ANOTHER ROUND

Bet your fellow bar bud that his glass is bigger around the top than it is tall. Measure it. A paper napkin or a string will do nicely. Measure the circumference around the top, then the height of the glass. The circumference will be larger, and you can drink to the marvels of geometry.

William Jaggers, a Scottish engineer, won $180,000 from the Monte Carlo casino in the late 1800s. After five weeks of obervations, Jaggers discovered that one of the roulette wheels was defective, resulting in certain numbers coming up more than others. Once management found out about it, they changed the wheel and that ended his winning streak. These days, casinos check and balance their wheels every 24 hours.

"There are two great pleasures in gambling: that of winning and that of losing."

-French Proverb

"Chance favors only a mind that is prepared."

-Louis Pasteur

Riley was quite the gambler. He got into a craps game one night and was up four thousand dollars after playing for a couple of hours. He decided to go for broke on his last bet - and lost everything. The shock was so tremendous that he had a massive heart attack and dropped dead.

The guys he was playing with had to figure out how to tell Riley's wife the news. One of them went to tell her. He knocked on the door and said, "Riley was playing craps with me and the boys at the casino tonight."

"That no good louse!" she said. "I told him he should never gamble."

"Well, he did - and, in fact, he won four thousand dollars."

"Oh my gosh!"

"But then he bet it all on the next roll of the dice and he lost."

"You mean he lost all the money?"

"I'm afraid so."

"That idiot! He should drop dead!"

"He did."

Maybe you've heard about the horse named Slowpoke. He was so slow that he came in last in the fifth race, but finished first in the sixth.

One racehorse bumps into another racehorse in the paddock. The first one says to the second, "Gee, your pace is familiar, but I don't remember your mane."

Baccarat was introduced to America in 1959 at the Sands Hotel-Casino in Las Vegas. On the very first day, two high rolling Texans won almost a quarter of a million dollars. The rules were quickly changed within 24 hours, reducing the player's advantage. The revised rules became the foundation for the American version of baccarat.

"If you are going to bluff, make it a big one."

-Amarillo Slim
(Thomas Austin Preston, Jr.)

"Millions of words are written annually purporting to tell how to beat the races, whereas the best possible advice on the subject is found in the three monosyllables: 'Do not try.'"

-Dan Parker

Paul-Son Gaming Supplies, an outfit in Las Vegas, makes 25,000 pairs of dice each month. Their dice are manufactured to a tolerance of 0.0003 inches. Casinos typically change all the dice at the beginning of each shift.

Oswald came home from a hard night of poker only to be met by his nagging wife.

"Where have you been?" she demanded.

"I've been out playing poker and I have some bad news. Pack your bags- I lost you in the last pot."

"You lost me in the last pot?!? How could you let that happen?"

"It wasn't easy," Oswald replied with a grimace, "I had to fold with a royal flush."

A man asked his doctor if he thought he might live to be a hundred. The doctor answered with the usual questions, "Do you smoke or drink?" The man happily replied, "No, I don't."

Next, the doctor inquired, "Do you drive fast cars or fool around?" Again, happily the man answered no.

"How about a Friday night poker game with the guys?" the doctor asked.

"Nope. Absolutely no gambling."

With a shrug of his shoulders and a shake of his head the doctor asked, "So with no smoking, drinking, fooling around or gambling, why the heck do you want to live to be 100?"

Roulette is a French word meaning "small wheel." The game evolved from pocketed wheel games that were played in England and continental France in the 18th century.

"One should always play fairly when one has the winning cards."

-Oscar Wilde

"A Smith & Wesson beats four aces."

-American Proverb

More than 100 million decks of cards are sold in the United States every year.

The joker in a deck of playing cards originated in America and first appeared about 1865.

Bar Bets

THE OLD SALT SHAKER

Pour a generous amount of salt in a pile on the bar. Then balance the salt shaker at a 45 degree angle on top of it. After the proper balance, gently blow away most of the pile, leaving only the very nitty-gritty grains to support the shaker. When your friend shows up, be sure to bet that he can't duplicate what you did: balance a salt shaker on a 45 degree angle while on a tiny pile on salt. Betcha he can't do it. By the way, be sure to leave the bartender a nice tip for cleaning up the mess.

POKER ODDS

Hand	# Of Possibilities	Probability
Royal flush (A, K, Q, J, 10 of same suit)	4	1 in 649,740
Straight flush (e.g., 8, 7, 6, 5, 4 of same suit)	36	1 in 72,193
Four of a kind (e.g., four fives)	624	1 in 4,165
Full house (three of a kind plus a pair)	3,744	1 in 694
Flush (any five cards of same suit)	5,108	1 in 509
Straight	10,200	1 in 255
Three of a kind	54,912	1 in 47
Two pair	123,552	1 in 21
One pair	1,098,240	1 in 2
No pair	1,302,540	1 in 2

"I'm on such a losing streak that if I had been around I would have taken General Custer and given points."
                                                -Joe E. Lewis

"The gambling known as business looks with disfavor upon the business known as gambling."

-Ambrose Bierce

The Big Six Wheel, also called the Wheel of Fortune or the Money Wheel, is one of the biggest long shots in the casino. The house edge start at 11 percent and can go as high as 24 percent.

A guy ran up to the bar from the poker room in the back and ordered twelve shots. They were lined up and he started knocking them back as fast as he could.

The bartender asked, "Say Pal, why are you drinking so fast?"

The guy replied, "You'd be drinking fast too if you had what I have."

The bartender looked at him curiously, "And what is it that you have?"

Drinking down the last shot, the man licked his lips and answered, "An empty wallet."

Harry was speeding home from the poker game at about three in the morning when he was pulled over by Clancy, the traffic cop.

"And where do you think you're going so fast?" asked Clancy.

"I'm late for the big lecture," Harry answered.

"And who might be giving a lecture at this hour?" Clancy asked suspiciously.

Harry looked Clancy right in the eye and replied, "My wife."

Horse-racing regulations require that no horse's name be longer than eighteen letters as any moniker longer than that would be too cumbersome on a racing sheet.

"I met with an accident on the way to the track. I arrived safely."

-Joe E. Lewis

"The only man who makes money following the races is one who does it with a broom and shovel."

-Elbert Hubbard

The game of choice for the World Series of Poker, held annually at Binion's Horseshoe Casino in Las Vegas, is Texas hold 'em. The entry fee is $10,000, and more than 500 players compete.

Dr. Billings got a call one evening and his long-suffering wife sighed as he answered the phone. She knew the patients came before special plans.

"Hey, Hank- we need a fourth for poker," said Dr. Smith on the phone.

"I'll be right there," answered Dr. Billings putting on his best poker face before turning back around.

"Is it serious?" asked his wife.

"I'll say," Billings replied. "There are three doctors there already."

Bar Bets

BREADWINNER

This one will really bring home the dough. All you need for the ingredients is a white piece of bread. It must be white bread. Bet your buddy that he/she can't down the bread in less than a minute. Seems easy enough, right? Wrong. Once your victim begins to eat the bread, their mouth quickly dries up, making it very difficult to swallow. Oh, and remember, no liquids are allowed.

In casino card games, when table stakes are used, you're not allowed to dip into your wallet for more money during a hand.

"Bookie: a pickpocket who lets you use your own hands."

-Henry Morgan

"The horse I bet on was so late getting home, he tiptoed into the stable."

-Henny Youngman

The game of craps was developed on the Mississippi and other inland waterways during the steamboat era of the 1800s.

Three small Nevada casino owners met on an around-the-world cruise and the first one said, "I had a horrible fire- destroyed everything. Now the insurance company is paying for everything and that's why I'm here."

The second casino owner said, "I had a terrible explosion which wiped me out. Now the insurance company is paying for everything and that's why I'm here."

The third casino owner said, "What a coincidence. I had a terrific flood that destroyed everything. Now the insurance company is paying for everything and that's why I'm here."

Confused, the other casino owners turned to him and said "Flood? How do you start a flood?"

Little Johnny dreamed of going to the zoo and pestered his parents about it day in and day out.

Finally his mother nagged his reluctant father into taking Johnny to the zoo for the day.

"So how was it?" his mother asked when they got home.

"Terrific," the father replied. "We had a great time. I was surprised at how much I enjoyed it."

"Is that true Johnny?" his mom asked. "Did Daddy really have as good a time as you?"

"Yeah, Mom ...He sure did- especially when one of the animals came running home at thirty to one!"

In 100 hands of blackjack, mathematically, the house will win 48 hands, the player will win 44, and there will be eight tie hands.

"The only game I like to play is Old Maid - provided she's not too old."

-Groucho Marx

"They love their gambling in Atlantic City.
I saw a guy putting a quarter in the parking
meter. I said, 'Are you crazy?'
He said, "Look at the odds - 8 to 5.""

-Bob Hope

There's a 1 in 20 chance of being dealt a blackjack in the game so-named.

Pro player Sam Bristol had spent six months
on the poker tournament circuit trying to make a
place for himself in the World Series of Poker.
Upon his return, he was anxious to make up for
lost time with his wife.

The reunion went well and they eventually fell
into a deep sleep around midnight.

An hour or so later, a knock at the door startled
them from their deep slumber.

"Oh my God! It's your husband," Sam
exclaimed.

"It can't be," came his wife's groggy reply. "He's
in Vegas playing poker."

TRIVIA TEST

1. In blackjack, players hope for a 21. What's the ultimate count sought in baccarat?

2. How many numbered sections is a standard roulette wheel divided into in the United States?

3. Charles Goren devised the point count bidding system for what card game?

4. What is an "ambsace?"

5. Killer Trivia: What was the name of the rock group for which Michael Bolton served as lead singer before he embarked on a solo career?

5. Blackjack.
4. Double aces - the lowest throw at dice.
3. Bridge.
2. 38.
1. Nine.

Las Vegas gives out about $2 million per day in comps.

"We won! We won! We won! Um, unfortunately, I bet on the other team, so we won't be going for pizza."

-Chief Clancy Wiggum
("The Simpsons")

*"I follow the horses. And the horses I follow,
follow the horses."*

-Joe E. Lewis

The oldest known game of chance in which dice were used was in 1573 BC by the Egyptians. If you're so inclined, you can see these Theban dice (as they are known today) in the Egyptian Museum in Berlin, Germany.

Bar Bets

DROP-A-DOLLAR (CHEAP SOBRIETY TEST)

Hold a crisp new dollar between your thumb and forefinger and challenge your chump that he cannot catch it when dropped.

Hold the bill right in the middle, right where Washington's head is.

When let go, the bill falls so fast that it will slip right through his fingers. Now it's your turn. You bet that you can catch it. How?

When you do it, you put your fingers at the bottom of the bill. It's easier to catch two-thirds of a bill rather than half. You have more time to grab it before it falls to the floor! It really has nothing to do with sobriety.

Practice makes perfect so do this trick a few times before betting… It'll help save you a buck.

The poker game was still going hot and heavy at two in the morning when one of the players returned to the table with news for the host.

"Hey Charlie," the guy said. "I was just coming back from the bathroom when I noticed Bill in the bedroom with your wife and they were kissing. I think you better get up there fast before something happens."

"Okay guys," said Charlie, "you heard him—this is positively the last deal."

Casino managers categorize players in different ways. The biggest high rollers in the world are known as "whales"; those who bet $100 to $250 a hand are "high rollers"; "median rollers" bet about $25 a hand; and "low rollers" are players who bet $3 to $10.

"Gambling: That's throwing money away while other people cheer you on."

-Steve Heldt

"Casino gambling is strange. You put down five dollars. They spin the wheel, take your money, and tell you what a good time you're having."

-Geoff Scowcroft

The "shoe" in blackjack was first introduced in Cuba in the early 1950s. Cuban dealers got to be very skilled at handling the cards. In order to prevent them from being too helpful to their friends at the table, casino managers introduced the dealing box known today as the shoe.

The gambler was so ecstatic at having bet on a 100 to one longshot which won the race that he rushed over to the winner's circle and planted a big kiss on the horse's face. The snooty owner of the horse frowned upon the gambler and said, "I say, Security...remove this man from the premises. How dare you do that to my horse!"

The gambler retorted, "I'm terribly sorry, my jolly good fellow. I thought it was your wife!"

In Heaven, Albert Einstein was welcoming his three new cloud-mates.

He greeted the first man and asked "What's your IQ?"

The man answered "198."

"Splendid!" Einstein answered. "We shall discuss the Grand Unification Theory and debate philosophy every Monday."

Einstein then asked the next man for his IQ.

"139," the man answered.

"Wonderful!" Einstein exclaimed. "We shall spend many happy hours discussing art and music on Wednesday nights."

Einstein then asked the third man his IQ.

The man strained to remember, then brightened up and said "47."

"47?" Einstein said, eyeing the man up. "All right then-poker every Friday!"

89 % of all visitors to Las Vegas gamble with an average gambling budget of $500.

"I used to be a heavy gambler. Now I just make mental bets. That's how I lost my mind."

-Steve Allen

"I don't get no respect. I joined Gamblers Anonymous. They gave me two to one I don't make it."

-Rodney Dangerfield

In terms of actual paid attendance, horse racing is the most popular sport in the world.

At an all-night truck stop, some long-haul drivers were sitting at a booth waiting for their burgers.

Big Bubba pulled out a deck of cards and suggested a few hands of poker to fill the time.

"But what are we gonna use for chips?" asked Snowman.

"We'll use these sweetener packets on the table," suggested Lazy Rider.

"But some are blue and some are pink," observed Mud-Flaps Mike. "Are they worth different amounts?"

"No," Big Bubba smiled. "They're Equal."

Bar Bets

LIP TRIPPER

It is well known that the convivial atmosphere of a bar loosens tongues. Well a tongue would need to be loose enough to tie a cherry stem in a sheepshank knot to even attempt this tongue twister. Betcha can't say "Unique New York" five times fast.

Here's something to think about while you're at the craps table. Supposedly, if you rub a pair of dice on a red-headed person it will bring good luck. (To you, not them.)

"According to statistics, it's a lot easier to get hit by lightning than to win a Lotto jackpot. The good side: You don't hear from your relatives."

-Johnny Carson

"I love blackjack, but I'm not addicted to gambling. I'm addicted to sitting in a semicircle."

                              -Mitch Hedberg

Dealers in United Kingdom casinos are not allowed to take tips from players.

A pinch-faced old lady was toddling down the street on her way home from church when she passed the local bookie joint.

Inspired by the sermon that she had just heard, she threw the door open and yelled at the startled gamblers.

"Pray for forgiveness!" she shouted. "Pray for forgiveness."

With that, she shut the door and continued home. A half a block later, an out-of-breath man caught up to her wheezing "I heard what you said- 'pray for forgiveness'."

The old woman was quite pleased with herself that her words had been heeded.

"But you didn't say, " the man continued, "which race?"

GAMBLERS ANONYMOUS

A selection of unattributed quotes

"If gambling is a disease, can you deduct your losses as a medical expense?"

"Playing with dice is a shaky business."

"A slot machine is a steel trap for catching dumb animals."

"The worst evil of gambling is that the odds are always with the house."

"The most deceptive mistress of all is Lady Luck."

"A visitor to Las Vegas received the "cook's tour" - he was baked in the sun, stewed at the bar, and burned at the crap tables."

"Every man has three secret wishes - to outsmart racehorses, women, and fish."

"Your typical Las Vegas vacation - out by jet, back in debt."

"Casino players are divided into two groups – the 'haves' and the 'hads'."

"The Native Americans say that gambling hasn't affected their native culture. I heard that directly from Chief Double Down."

-Buzz Nutley

"Americans spend three hundred billion dollars every year on games of chance, and that doesn't even include weddings and elections."

-Argus Hamilton

Mansour Matloubi, the 1990 champion of the World Series of Poker at Binion's Horseshoe in Las Vegas, walked away with $1,022,400- tax-free! Why? Matloubi was from London. As such, there is no tax on gambling wins in the United Kingdom, and the U.S. treaty with the U.K. exempts taxation of money won by British citizens in the U.S.

And then there was the horse named Flea Bag... He never won any races because he kept getting scratched.

A family of three from the remote South Pacific island of Poomba-Poomba, were visiting Las Vegas. They had just walked into the MGM Grand when the woman paused to admire the lobby. The father and son went on ahead and for the first time in their lives saw an elevator.

They were perplexed by the sideways sliding doors and couldn't imagine what the little room was for. Just then, an elderly woman walked up and hit the button. The doors opened and she stepped in. The boy and his dad watched as the doors closed and the little round numbers went higher and higher. Then they paused and dropped back down. A little bell sounded, the doors opened and out stepped a voluptuous, eighteen-year old beauty.

The father seemed quite amazed and tapped his son on the shoulder. "Boy," he said intently, "go get your mother."

"When a man tells me he's going to put all his cards on the table, I always look up his sleeve."

-Lord Leslie Hore-Belisha

"When a gambler picks up a pack of cards or a pair of dice, he feels as though he has reduced an unmanageable world to a finite, visible and comprehensive size."

- Annabel Davis-Goff,
"The Literary Companion to Gambling"

It's against the law in Nevada to knowlingly take advantage of a defective video or slot machine by playing it.

Q: What do you call a fellow who's taken courses in how to fish and how to gamble?
A: A reeler dealer.

Did you hear the one about the guy who was know as "The Exorcist" at the weekly poker game?
That's because once he shows up, all the spirits disappear.

"I know a little bit about handicapping. If the horse has an IV, you want to stay away from it."

-Paula Poundstone

In addition to legalized casino gambling, one of Atlantic City's attractions include the first boardwalk in the country, built in 1870.

CARD CAPERS

Thirteen is a pretty rotten hand to be dealt in blackjack, but it's a pretty good number for this card trick.

Pre-stack the top of a deck of cards with the six of hearts, seven of diamonds, six of diamonds and seven of hearts, in that order. Have your subject take a look at the top two cards and instruct him or her to place them anywhere in the deck. Next, you shuffle the deck, making sure to leave the the top two cards (six of diamonds and seven of hearts) in tact. Now have your subject take a look at the top two cards and ask if they're the original ones. It works every time...well, most of the time...well, some of the time.

"Look around the table. If you don't see a sucker, get up, because you're the sucker."

-Amarillo Slim

Some casinos use three or five decks in blackjack. The reason for the unusual number is to make card-counting more difficult.

Charlie came home after a terrible night of poker. With a scowl, he flopped down on the couch and told his wife, "Get me a beer before it starts."

She sighed, but fetched him a beer.

Five minutes later he snapped, "Get me another beer before it starts."

His better half was annoyed, but got him the beer anyway.

Charlie knocked that one back and said, "Quick- one more- it's going to start any minute."

That did it. His wife let loose. "You've been out playing poker all evening. Now you come home and you think all you're going to do is drink beer and watch TV? You're just a drunken slob."

With that, Charlie sighed and said, "It's started already."

Q: What's the difference between a guy who plays poker but doesn't think he's very good at it and Bigfoot?

A: Somebody has actually seen Bigfoot.

Q: What single word can make a roomful of little old ladies swear?

A: "Bingo!"

From 1943 to 1945 Richard M. Nixon, then a U.S. Navy Lieutenant, won more than $6,000 playing poker while assigned as a supply officer in the South Pacific during WWII. He used those winnings to finance a victorious campaign for the U.S. House of Representatives in 1946.

"If you want to cure a compulsive gambler, give him the Cincinnati Bengals and four points."

-Jeff Kreismer

"No horse can go as fast as the money you bet on him."

-Nate Collier

A sad looking little guy was sitting at a casino bar just staring blankly at his drink.

After a while, a big guy swaggered in with a girl on each arm. He announced that he just hit the slots for a million bucks and wanted to celebrate.

Muscling the little guy aside, he snatched his drink and belted it down.

"Thanks for the drink, loser," he laughed derisively.

At that, the little man burst into tears.

"What are you caterwauling about?" groused Mr. Big Shot.

"Well," said the little man, "my business recently went under, my son disowned me and this afternoon, I came home to find my wife cheating on me. And now..." his voice broke.

"Yeah, and now what?" the bully sneered.

"And now just as I'm sitting here trying to get up enough courage to end my life, you come along and drink my poison."

Bar Bets

CAN'T WIN FOR LOSING

All you need for this bar bet is a genial victim who has just had a drink served, a napkin and a straw. Drop the napkin over the glass so that it's completely covered.

"I'll bet you a buck that I can drink your entire drink without touching it." While they gaze suspiciously at the straw add, "No, I won't touch the straw either."

Assure them that you won't touch anything.

As soon as they agree, pick up the glass and knock back their hooch.

"I guess you were right," you say, pushing over your dollar wager in return for a four-dollar drink.

The oldest casino in the world, where people have been gambling for more than 200 years, is in Baden-Baden, Germany

"I must complain the cards are ill-shuffled, 'till I have a good hand."

-Jonathan Swift, English satirist

"Beware, above all, of the man who simply tells you he broke even. He is the big winner."

-Anthony Holden

The game of poker as we know it today was developed in the U.S. in the early 1800s.

Jasper stood accused of cheating at cards and was handling his own defense.

"Your Honor," he began, "my arm was holding the offending cards and my arm is guilty as charged but is it fair to imprison the whole person for a crime committed by a single body part?"

The judge was amused by the creativity of the defense and ruled. "Your argument is well taken. I hereby sentence your arm to one year in state prison. I'll leave it up to you whether you choose to accompany it or not."

"Fair enough, Your Honor," the gambler replied. "Get out the cuffs!" he said as he handed the bailiff his prosthetic arm.

Did you hear the one about the guy who went to Las Vegas for some change and rest? The bellhops took the change and the casino took the rest.

And then there was the gambler who was so unlucky he once caught athlete's foot from the pool at Lourdes.

In 1997, Maria Stern won the World Series of Poker seven-card stud event and Max Stern won the seven-card stud high-low event. They became the first husband and wife to win World Series of Poker titles.

"Nobody is always a winner, and anybody who says he is, is either a liar or doesn't play poker."

-Amarillo "Slim" Preston

"Poker is a tough way to make an easy living."

-Poker Wisdom

George Washington owned a number of horses which he raced in Alexandria and Annapolis.

A horse shows up at an open tryout for the New York Yankees. The manager doesn't take the horse too seriously, but nonetheless, allows him to take some swings in the batting cage. Much to his surprise, the horse is an unbelievable power hitter and after clubbing ten homers in a row the Yankees decide to sign him up.

That night, the horse is sitting on the bench. In the bottom of the ninth, with two men out and the Yankees trailing 2-1, the horse is called on to pinch-hit. He steps up to the plate, cracks the first pitch off the centerfield wall and just stands there.

Everyone in the dugout is standing and yelling, "Run! Run!"

The horse says, "Run! Hrrmmmmmph! If I could run, I'd be at Belmont!"

And then there was the bookie who changed his name to Red Cross so his customers' losses would be tax deductible.

The British have always been betting and gambling buffs. It's in accordance with their idea of sports and sportsmanship - basically a British philosophy. But the Earl of Sandwich (1718-1792) overdid it even by British standards. During his gambling days, taking meals was considered by him as highly unwelcome interruptions. He therefore invented a kind of meal not requiring him to exchange the gaming table for the dining table: sandwiches.

"Poker among friends and colleagues should not drive anyone to the poorhouse but gaming is common, though a passion for keeping roulette tables is unknown."

-George Bernard Shaw

"A thing worth having is a thing worth cheating for."

\- W.C. Fields

The Nevada Gaming Commission reports that casinos are earning about a 16-percent return at craps.

Bar Bets

THAT'S THE LAST STRAW!

Take six straws and put them in a house shape- that is, a triangle for the roof and three straws enclosing a box under it.

The challenge here is to make four more-or-less even triangles by moving only three straws.

The reason this one is a sure winner and a crowd pleaser (except maybe for the guy who loses the bet) is that it has a simple, elegant but three-dimensional solution. Pick up the three straws that form the "walls" of the house and stand them up just inside the "roof" triangle. You will probably have to hold them together at the apex but you will have four roughly equal triangles nonetheless. Another sure bet is that the other guy will wish he'd studied geometry harder at school!

TRIVIA TEST

1. Name the horse that was the last winner of the Triple Crown?

2. How many dots are there on a pair of dice?

3. In poker, a pair of aces and a pair of eights is known as the Dead Man's Hand. How did it get its name?

4. By what name was Dimitrios Synodinos better known in the gambling world?

5. Among card players, who is the pone?

5. The person sitting to the dealer's right.
4. Jimmy "the Greek" Snyder, the renowned oddsmaker.
in Deadwood, South Dakota, in 1876.
gunned down during a card game at the Nuttal and Mann Saloon
3. It was the hand Wild Bill Hickok was holding when he was
2. 42
1. Affirmed, in 1978.

"Pari-mutuel," as in the racetrack bet, is French for "to wager amongst ourselves."

"My horse finished so far back, the jockey had to run ahead of him with a flashlight."

-Bob Hope

"Baccarat is a game whereby the croupier gathers in money with a flexible sculling oar, then rakes it home. If I could have borrowed his oar I would have stayed."
-Mark Twain

Hey, you know that famous picture of Napoleon Bonaparte with his hand under his vest? Well, that may be because he was holding some cards up his sleeve. It's well documented that he loved the game of blackjack.

The handsome young man had just broken the bank at roulette in Atlantic City and was collecting his winnings when a beautiful woman sidled up to him.

"You look just like my fourth husband," she purred.

"Fourth husband?" he replied. "How many times have you been married?"

"Three," she smiled.

A husband was reading the paper when his wife smacked him in the head with a rolled up magazine.

"What was that for?" he whined.

"I was just getting your clothes ready for the cleaners and I found a paper in your pocket with the name Kimberly and a phone number."

"But Honey," he replied, "Kimberly is the name of a horse I had a tip on the last time I went to the track. The digits are the race, the horse's number and the odds."

"Oh dear, can you ever forgive me?" the wife pleaded. "Jealousy makes me act so silly."

"Well, okay, I guess I can let you slide this time seeing as how you're just a woman and all," the husband answered condescendingly.

An hour later, he was reading his paper again when his wife came up and hit him over the head with the phone.

"What'd you do that for?" he demanded.

His wife gave him a dirty look and said, "Your horse called."

"At the gambling table, there are no fathers and sons."

\- Chinese Proverb

"A lottery is a salutary instrument and a tax laid on the willing only, that is to say, on those who can risk the price of a ticket without sensible injury, for the possibility of a higher prize."

- Thomas Jefferson

The superstition that seven is a lucky number comes from the game of craps. As you probably know if you're reading this book, if you roll a seven on the first try, you win.

O'Toole was hard at it at the blackjack table when something brushed his knee. He looked down to see a leprechaun.

"Leave the table," the leprechaun said, "and I'll take you to me pot of gold. It'll be more riches than you can spend in three lifetimes."

"Okay, Okay," O'Toole mumbled. "Just let me get even first."

Bar Bets

IF THEY'RE SUSAN, THEY'RE LOSIN'

Here's a bar bet that can be won with a couple of Susan B. Anthony dollars- the coins that resemble quarters.

Set two Suzie B's on the bar heads up and ask your mark what they see.

They'll probably say "two dollars" or "two heads" or something on that order.

Squint and say that you see two quarters. They'll insist that the coins are dollars. Now say "I'm pretty sure they're quarters. If I'm wrong will you buy me a drink?" Usually they'll say "Sure!" That's when you just admit, in fact, that you are wrong and enjoy the refreshment.

In 1987, Joseph P. Crowley won $3 million in the Ohio lottery. He retired to Boca Raton, Florida, six years later and played the Florida Lotto on Christmas Day in 1993. He won $20 million.

"I bet on a horse at ten-to-one. It didn't come in until half-past five. "

- Henny Youngman

"Horse racing is animated roulette."

-Roger Kahn

In the Rainbow Room, high above New York City, two guys were standing at the bar when the first guy bet the second $100 that he could jump out the window and come right back in, unharmed. The second guy took the bet and so the first guy jumped out the window and just floated in mid-air.

Astonished, the second guy bet that he couldn't do it again but sure enough, the first guy repeated the stunt.

The second guy really wanted to get his money back and, figuring that a gust of wind must be blowing up the side of the skyscraper, he bet the first guy $1,000 that he too could jump out the window and return a few seconds later unharmed. The first guy took the bet and even opened the window for the second guy, who finished his drink and confidently leapt out into thin air. He immediately fell over fifty stories to his death.

The bartender, who had been holding the wagers, shook his head as he handed the money over and said, "You know, you get really nasty when you've been drinking, Superman."

THREE LAWS OF POKER

Accept the fact that some days you are the pigeon and some days you are the statue.

Luck always seems to go against those who depend on it.

Don't gamble unless you can afford to lose, and if you can afford to lose, you don't have to gamble.

Maude: *"My husband's going to a casino in a remote part of central Asia."*
Mabel: *"Tibet?"*
Maude: *"Of course, why else would he go?"*

Did you hear the one about the young man who said to his girlfriend, "I bet you won't marry me." She not only called his bet but she raised him five.

"Gambling itself will only end when human nature has changed completely and there are no more bets to win."

- Harold S. Smith, Sr.

"Last night I stayed up late playing poker with Tarot cards. I got a full house and four people died."

- Steven Wright

In 1732, Benjamin Franklin advertised the sale of playing cards in his first Poor Richard's Almanac.

On September 5, 1770, George Washington's diary entry read, "At home all day playing cards."

A high roller had cashed in his chips in Vegas and a few of his gambling cronies were gathered at his graveside.

The minister intoned reassuringly "Sid is merely sleeping."

From the back his best friend ,Al, was heard to mutter ,"I've got a c-note that says he's dead."

CHANCE REMARKS

"You know what luck is? Luck is believing you're lucky...
to hold front position in this rat-race you've got to
believe you're lucky."
> *- Stanley Kowalski,*
> *"A Streetcar Named Desire"*

"Luck never gives; it only lends."
> *- Swedish Proverb*

"It is the mark of an inexperienced man not to believe in luck."
> *- Joseph Conrad*

"My lucky number is four billion, which usually doesn't come
in handy when you're gambling. 'Come on four billion...'"
> *-Mitch Hedberg*

"Talk about bad luck. I once drew four aces in a poker
game and won $12,000 worth of counterfeit money."
> *-Tom Lehmann*

"At gambling, the deadly sin is to mistake bad play for
bad luck."
> *-Ian Fleming*

"Luck is a mighty queer thing. All you know about it for
certain is that it's bound to change."
> *-Bret Harte*

"Luck is the residue of design."
> *-Branch Rickey*

"She got to go to heaven four days early."

> - President Bill Clinton,
> noting his mother's visit to
> Las Vegas the weekend
> before she died

A Braille slot machine was patented in 1994. Micro-computer technology was used to read the symbols coming up on the machine's dials and translate them into raised Braille images.

Bar Bets

OLIVE A GOOD TRICK

Here's one that might require a bit of practice:

The bet is that you can get an olive on the bar into a brandy snifter without touching it or rolling it off the bar in any way.

Simply place the snifter over the olive with the inside edge against the olive. Now rotate the glass so that the olive rolls around inside the snifter faster and faster. Eventually, it will be going so fast that you'll have time to flip the snifter upright.

Fred and Irma rarely went out but on their twentieth anniversary, they decided to pull out all the stops.

They went down the shore to an Atlantic City casino but the next day, Irma was bitterly complaining to their next door neighbor.

"We needed something to eat before hitting the slots so went over to the buffet," she said to her friend.

"We walked in and saw a sign that said 'Please wait for hostess to be seated.' Fred and I stood there all night and that girl never did sit down."

According to gambling odds expert Mike Orkin, a winning roulette system is impossible. In repeated play, you're certain to lose, your long-run losses averaging 5.3 cents per dollar bet.

"Fortune knocks at every man's door once in a lifetime, but in a good many cases the man is in a neighboring saloon and does not hear her."

- Mark Twain

"The subject of gambling is all encompassing. It combines man's natural play instinct with his desire to know about his fate and his future."

-Franz Rosenthal,
Gambling in Islam

There are 2,598,960 possible poker hands with a fifty-two card deck.

A woman won thirty million dollars in the lottery but was afraid to tell her husband for fear that he'd drop dead of a heart attack. She went to her minister for advice as to how to tell him. "Not to worry... I'll take him to lunch and find a way to break it to him gently."

The minister and the woman's husband went to lunch whereupon the clergyman said, "You know, a lot of people are winning the lottery these days. What would you do if you won that thirty million dollar jackpot?"

The man responded, "Well, first, I would give you and the church half of the winnings," at which point the minister dropped dead of a heart attack.

A thoroughly sloshed slot player stumbled into the casino lounge, staggered up to a woman at the bar and planted a big, wet, sloppy kiss right on her lips.

With that, the woman slapped him in the face, bringing him to his senses.

"Awfully sorry old girl," he said rubbing his cheek, "But you look exactly like my wife."

"You know you're a worthless, drunken, useless excuse for a human being," she snarled.

"Come to think of it," slurred the old inebriate, "you sound exactly like her as well."

The name of the bugle tune as the horses parade onto the Kentucky Derby race-track is *A Call to the Post.*

"Italians come to ruin most generally in three ways- women, gambling, and farming. My family chose the slowest one."

- Pope John XXIII

"I can't believe my rotten luck," moaned Mulligan. "I haven't had a winning horse in more than two months."

"Hey, maybe you should try out my system," said Hoolihan. "It's worked pretty well for me lately."

"What system is that?" asked Mulligan.

"Well," answered Hoolihan, "it's pretty simple. Every day that I plan on going to the track, that morning I go to church and pray for ten minutes. I've had at least two winners a day since I've been doing that."

Mulligan was ready to try anything so, sure enough, the next morning he went to church and prayed for half an hour. Then it was off to the racetrack. At the end of the day, he ran into Hoolihan.

"That system of yours is patooie!" he complained to Hoolihan. "I went to church this morning, prayed three times as long as you do and didn't have a single winner all afternoon."

"Where did you go to church?" asked Hoolihan.

"To the one on Peach Street," said Mulligan.

"You idiot!" exclaimed Hoolihan. "That church is for trotters."

Bar Bets

TAKE A SHOT

The bet is that you can drink three pints of beer before your buddy can down one shot. The only thing is that you get a one-beer head start and neither can touch the other's glass. Also, your victim can't pick up his glass until you put your first one down. Have the drinks set up, drink your first beer and then put the mug upside-down over the shot glass. Take your time and enjoy your other beers- and victory.

Movie star John Wayne won the famed dog Lassie from his owner and trainer in a poker game in 1955. The Duke was kind enough to give the dog back.

"In the case of an earthquake hitting Las Vegas, be sure to go straight to the keno lounge. Nothing ever gets hit there."

- An anonymous casino boss

"Remember this: The house doesn't beat the player. It just gives him the opportunity to beat himself."

- Nicholas (Nick the Greek) Dandalos

The most commonly played number combinations in lotteries are:

01-02-03-04-05-06

07-14-21-28-35-42

05-10-15-20-25-30

The six consecutive numbers of 1-2-3-4-5-6 have never been drawn in any U.S. or international lottery game.

The difference between a horse race and a political race is that in a horse race, the front end of the horse wins.

A guy sat at a bar drinking one afternoon and ran up quite a bar tab.

Finally, he said to the bartender, "I bet you my bar bill, double or nothing, that I can bite my eye."

Seeing easy money from someone with obviously impaired judgment, the bartender agreed.

With that, the man took out a glass eye and nipped it before popping it back in.

The bartender fumed, but honored the bet and the man kept drinking.

A while later, the guy said to the bartender, "I'll bet you my bar bill, double or nothing that I can bite my other eye."

This time, the bartender knew he had him. He saw him walk in- he knew he wasn't blind. "He can't have two glass eyes!" the bartender thought. "Okay, I'll take that bet," the bartender said smugly.

And with that, the guy popped out his dentures and took a little nip on his other eye.

"A race track is a place where windows clean people."

- Danny Thomas

"All life is 6-5 against."

-Damon Runyon

A Texan swaggered into a pub in Ireland and loudly announced, "I'll give one thousand dollars to the man who can knock back ten pints of Guinness, one right after another."

There was a silence in the pub. One guy even got up and ran out.

"Ha!" the Texan snorted. "I thought so- and you Irish are supposed to be such great drinkers."

Twenty minutes later, the man who had run out came back and asked the Texan if the offer was still good.

"Sure," the Texan crowed. "Set 'em up!"

The Irishman stepped up to the bar and guzzled down the pints, one after another and finished in just over a minute.

The Texan was amazed as he counted out the money. "Well I guess you Irish can drink after all," he said. "But if you don't mind me asking, where did you go for that twenty minutes?"

"Oh, down the street to Clancy's Pub," the Irishman replied. "I just wanted to be sure I could do it first."

GAMBLERS ANONYMOUS

A selection of unattributed quotes

"Las Vegas is the land of the spree, and the home of the knave."

"A lot of people who wouldn't bet on a horse turn around and get married."

"An ace in the hand is worth two in the deck."

"My idea of royalty is a pair of jacks or better."

"To a gambler, the largest diamond is the ace."

"I gambled away the rent money. It was a moving experience."

"In playing cards, a good deal depends on a good deal."

"The best way to conceal your hand in poker is with your face."

"Odds are you won't get even."

Hawaii and Utah are the only states which don't have any form of legal public gambling or private charity gambling.

"A gambler is nothing but a man who makes his living out of hope." -William Bolitho

"A number of moralists condemn lotteries and refuse to see anything noble in the passion of the ordinary gambler. They judge gambling as some atheists judge religion, by its excesses."

-Charles Lamb,
Essays of Elia, 1832

In Texas hold'em you'll be dealt an ace about 15% of the time. That's about one in six hands.

Bar Bets

FIRE MEETS ITS MATCH

Here's one that involves fire and, as such, requires adult supervision- ideally adults without flammable breath.

Fill a paper cup with water (paper-not foam of any kind). Bet that someone can't strike a match and burn through the bottom of the cup.

The reason this trick works is that the water in the cup cools the hotspot in the bottom keeping it below the ignition point. Warning: Choose your victim wisely or the match may not be the only thing that gets struck.

"You think so much of your old card playing that you don't even remember when we were married," complained the pouting wife.

"Of course I do, Honey. It was that day I got the straight flush."

The first book in America to mention the word "gambling" was *An Exposure of the Arts and Miseries of Gambling*, written by Jonathan H. Green in 1983.

The dots on a pair of dice are called pips.

"Even as I approach the gambling hall, as soon as I hear, two rooms away, the jingle of money poured out on the table, I almost go into convulsions."

    - Fyodor Dostoevsky,
    "*The Gambler*" (1867)

"He had the calm confidence of a Christian with four aces."

-Mark Twain

It was a slow night in the casino and the two dealers at the craps table were waiting for their first customers when a woman arrived and said she wanted to bet $10,000 on a single roll of the dice.

"Of course, ma'am," said one of the dealers.

"There's just one thing though," she said. "I hope you don't mind if I go topless because it always brings me luck."

She then stripped, rolled the dice and screamed, "I've won! I've won."

Then she scraped up the money, picked up her clothes and left.

The two dealers were flabbergasted. One said to the other, "What'd she roll, anyway?"

The other said, "I don't know. I thought you were watching the dice."

"Doc, I need help," says Mort to his
psychiatrist. *"It may sound strange but I keep
thinking that I'm a horse."*

"I think I can cure you," the psychiatrist
answers, *"but it's going to take some time and it's
going to be extremely expensive."*

*"Money's not a problem, Doc. I just won the
Kentucky Derby."*

Of the millions of dollars bet on sporting
events every year in Nevada, the "big three" -
football, baseball and basketball - garner
almost 92 percent of the wagers.

*Floyd: Doyle, I know I gave him four threes. He
had to make a switch. We can't let him get away
with that.*

*Doyle Lonnigan: What was I supposed to do --
call him for cheating better than me, in front of
the others?*
                              - "The Sting", 1973

"Suckers have no business with money anyway."

- Canada Bill Jones

In casino lingo, a "loose" slot machine is one that pays out more than others, which are called "tight" machines.

A man goes to the racetrack and sees a priest making the sign of the cross over a horse. The horse goes on to win the first race. Before the second race, the priest blesses another horse, and it too comes in first.

The man figures he'll follow suit. He bets on each horse the priest blesses.

When the last race comes up the priest makes the sign of the cross over a horse.

The man bets his whole fortune on the horse.

The race starts. The horse drops dead as it leaves the gate.

The man rushes to the priest and demands to know what went wrong.

The priest says, "Son, don't you know the difference between a blessing and the last rites?"

Bar Bets

SNEAKY THROUGH AND THROUGH

Here's an oldie but a goodie. Bet you can push a glass through the handle of a beer mug. Sounds impossible right? Well it would be were it not for the nebulous meaning of the word "through". Simply use your finger or a straw, slide it through the handle of the beer mug and push the glass.

The game of Bingo was originally known as Beano.

Las Vegas is Spanish for "the meadows."

"When we put 50 machines in, I consider them 50 more mousetraps. You have to have a mousetrap to catch a mouse."

- Bob Stupak, former
Las Vegas casino owner

A man walked into a casino lounge after being wiped out at the blackjack table.

The bartender said, "What'll it be?" and the man replied, "A scotch, please."

The bartender poured him the drink, and said, "That'll be five dollars."

The man said, "What are you talking about? I don't owe you anything for this."

A lawyer sitting a few stools down, advised the bartender, "He's got you there. In the original offer, which constitutes a binding contract upon acceptance, there was no stipulation of remuneration."

The irritated bartender said to the man, "Okay, you beat me for a drink. But don't ever let me catch you in here again".

The next day, the man walked back into the lounge after another evening of huge losses at blackjack.. The bartender said, "What the heck are you doing in here? I told you never to come back."

"What are you talking about?" the man asked oh-so-innocently. "I've never been in this place before in my life!"

"I bet," said the bartender, "You must have a double then."

"Thank you," the man smiled. "Make it a scotch."

RAMBLING ABOUT GAMBLING

Odds are you won't get all of these questions correctly.

1. What kind of animal was always the odds-on favorite to win The Irish Sweepstakes?

2. What's odd - or even odder than just plain odd - about all the numbers on a roulette wheel?

3. The Liberty Bell has a place in history but the name also had a central place in the annals of gambling. What is it?

4. In which sport did Aristides win the highest honor?

5. If you were in Los Angeles and decided to take in some of the action in Reno, which direction would you drive?

1. Humans...It was a national lottery began in 1930.
2. They add up to 666 - a number that many attribute to Satan.
3. It was the first modern slot machine, invented by Charles Fey in San Francisco in 1899.
4. He won the first Kentucky Derby in 1875.
5. Well, you could go north and east but if you actually wanted to get there, you'd have to drive north and west.

And then there was the horse that came in so late the jockey was wearing pajamas.

"Shallow men believe in luck. Strong men believe in cause and effect."
- Ralph Waldo Emerson

"Jed, only one man in a hundred plays poker by the odds. Luck's only important when you sit down with men who play as tight as you do. When I find that out, I quit. It's gambling."

- Bart Maverick

A TOAST TO GAMBLING

A little whiskey now and then
Is relished by the best of men;
It surely drives away dull care,
And makes ace high look like two pair.

A guy played a nickel and dime game of cards with Siamese twins. When asked if he won, he replied, "Yes and no."

Strip poker is the only game in the world where the more you lose, the more you have to show for it.

Q: How do you get a professional poker player off your porch?

A: Pay him for the pizza.

Q: What's the only creature that can take thousands of people for a ride at the same time?

A: A racehorse.

In 2003, 27-year old Chris Moneymaker, an accountant from Spring Hill, Tennessee, was the first World Series of Poker $10,000 Buy-in No-Limit Texas hold'em player to have won his entry fee through an on-line Texas hold'em tournament. His original buy-in was only $40.

"Someone once asked me why women don't gamble as much as men do, and I gave the common-sensical reply that we don't have as much money. That was a true but incomplete answer. In fact, women's total instinct for gambling is satisfied by marriage."

-Gloria Steinem

"The gambling known as business looks with austere disfavor upon the business known as gambling."

\- Ambrose Bierce

In the 1860s, a deck of cards was referred to as "The Devil's Picture Gallery" by preachers and anti-gambling proponents.

Bar Bets

BREATH TEST

This classic bar bet requires a dry beer bottle and a wadded up piece of dry napkin. The bet is that even the bar's biggest blowhards cannot blow the paper wadding from just inside the lip of the bottle, down past the neck and into the bottle.

In physics, they call it the Bernoulli Principle. In pubs, they call it the Barstoolie Principle- when a bet seems too easy to win, it usually is. The moving air has a lower pressure than the stationary air in the bottle so the paper should be blown right back out. They may huff and puff but the paper wad will stay stuck in the neck or blow out.

When dealing with Uncle Sam, you can only deduct your gambling losses against your winnings. And, if you're fortunate to be a winner, it is considered income in the U.S. by both state and federal governments.

A betting man died and left the world's shortest will. It read, "Being of sound mind, I spent my money."

"Stop cheating!" the dealer warned the card player.
"I'm not!" protested the player.
"Yes you are," said the dealer. "That is not the hand that I dealt you."

"Judged by the dollars spent, gambling is now more popular in America than baseball, the movies, and Disneyland combined."

- Timothy L. O'Brien,
"Bad Bet"

"As my dear old grandfather Litvak said (just before they swung the trap), 'You can't cheat an honest man. Never give a sucker an even break or smarten up a chump.'"

- W. C. Fields

Q: *What do you get when you cross a hen with a bookmaker?*

A: *A chicken that lays odds.*

Q: *How do you keep a gambler in suspense?*

A:

In 1610, the first known use of the word "deck" was made by William Shakespeare to describe what was then universally known as a pack of cards.

CARD CAPERS

This is one super duper, unbelievable, can't give enough superlatives to, card trick… Okay, here's what you need: two card decks, a large orange (preferably a navel orange with thick skin), knife, glue, and a pair of scissors.

Here's what you do: In preparation, carefully cut off the skin from the top of the orange so as not to destroy it. Then, take a card from one of the decks- we'll say the Ace of Diamonds. Snip off the top left corner of it. Roll the card as tightly as possible in cigarette fashion. Next, stuff the rolled-up card into the core of the orange. Once you've done that, glue the piece of orange you cut off back on to the top of it. Done properly, no one will be able to detect the orange had been tampered with. Dispose of the deck of cards from which you removed the Ace. Put the orange in a convenient place- the refrigerator, for instance. Take the other deck of cards and put the Ace of Diamonds on top. Now you're ready to do your thing. Shuffle the cards in front of your victim, but make sure to keep the Ace on top. Instruct him/her to take the top card (the Ace) and look at it but don't show it to you. Then ask to have the card back, face down. Take the card and cut the top left corner of it exactly as you did with the previous Ace. Give that corner of the card to your victim. Then proceed to cut up the rest of the card into little bits and pieces. Put it in your hand, and at a convenient time when no one can see, insert it in your pocket. Then, have your victim go to the spot where you've placed the orange. Either you or the victim can then peel the orange to reveal the Ace of Diamonds. The corner of it will be cut off just as it was on the other Ace, proof of the pudding that the victim's card had magically resurfaced! Trust us, it's great!!

"Too many people who disapprove of gambling want to ban it. It's not generally been the policy of the U.S. government to tell people how to spend their money."

- Rep. Barney Frank

Johnny Moss was the winner of the First World Series of Poker in Las Vegas in 1970. He won all five events, defeating a field of thirty-seven other players.

Bar Bets

A PENNY FOR YOUR THOUGHTS

Here's one where your mark is all wet. Demonstrate the trick first by wetting a penny and sticking it to your forehead. A furrow or two of the eyebrow and it will fall off. The bet? Do the same to your victim's forehead, but secretly remove the penny. The wet spot will convince them that the penny is there and they'll be puzzled as they make ever more contorted expressions trying to get the penny to drop. You may not win much but it's fun to watch!

"Hey Jim, these pretzels are stale!" the boisterous poker party guest complained to his host.

"No they're not, I bought them fresh this morning," Jim answered defensively.

"Oh yeah?" sneered his guest." Then how come the expiration date is in Roman Numerals?"

The United States Playing Card Company in Norwood, Ohio, is the world's largest manufacturer of playing cards. Their Bicycle brand has been in production since 1885.

Playing cards in India are round.

"When your opponent's sittin' there holdin' all the aces, there's only one thing to do: kick over the table."
                                        - Dean Martin

"Your best chance to get a Royal Flush in a casino is in the bathroom."

-Jack Kreismer